DATE DUE

MAR 1 9 2004		
AUG 3 0 2005		
JUN 2 8 2006		
AUG 0 1 2006		

Demco, Inc. 38-293

Inventions

FaQ

FrequentlyaskedQuestions

Written by Valerie Wyatt

Illustrated by Matthew Fernandes

Kids Can Press

For my niece and nephew, Laura Albert and Wyatt Mullin, with love

Acknowledgments

Every book, even the third in a series, is a new adventure. Fortunately, this series has the benefit of a highly skilled editorial and design team. Editor Liz MacLeod and designer Marie Bartholomew keep coming up with creative solutions and new ways to make each book the best it can be. Their talent — and their friendship — mean a lot to me. I also thank the others at Kids Can Press who provide great support for me in so many ways, especially Rivka Cranley, Valerie Hussey, Julia Naimska and Stacey Roderick. And, of course, I'm grateful to my husband, Larry, for his warm heart and keen mind.

Kids Can Press acknowledges the financial support of the Ontario Arts Council, the Canada Council for the Arts and the Government of Canada, through the BPIDP, for our publishing activity.

Published in Canada by
Kids Can Press Ltd.
29 Birch Avenue
Toronto, ON M4V 1E2

Published in the U.S. by
Kids Can Press Ltd.
2250 Military Road
Tonawanda, NY 14150

www.kidscanpress.com

Edited by Elizabeth MacLeod
Designed by Marie Bartholomew

Printed in Hong Kong, China, by Wing King Tong Company Limited

The hardcover edition of this book is smyth sewn casebound.
The paperback edition of this book is limp sewn with a drawn-on cover.

CM 03 0 9 8 7 6 5 4 3 2 1
CM PA 03 0 9 8 7 6 5 4 3 2 1

National Library of Canada Cataloguing in Publication Data

Wyatt, Valerie
Inventions / written by Valerie Wyatt ; illustrated by Matthew Fernandes.

(Frequently asked questions)
Includes index.

ISBN 1-55337-403-7 (bound).   ISBN 1-55337-404-5 (pbk.)

1. Inventions — Juvenile literature. I. Fernandes, Matthew II. Title. III. Series.

T48.W93 2002   j608   C2002-902606-7

Kids Can Press is a *Corus*™ Entertainment company

Contents

How Inventive

FaQ Why do people invent?

Have you ever had a shoelace that wouldn't stay tied, a sink full of dishes to wash or a jar of peanut butter that you couldn't get that last bit out of? Then you understand why inventors came up with Velcro, the dishwasher and a jar that can be opened from both ends.

Inventors invent to make things easier, better, faster, cheaper or even more fun, and they've been inventing for thousands of years. Some of their inventions — such as a bed with a built-in piano for sleepless musicians — never go anywhere. But many, such as the telephone, money, tin cans, computers and even pets, have changed the way we live. Read on to find answers to your Frequently Asked Questions about inventions.

FaQ

Do you need special training to become an inventor?

No. All you need is the ability to spot a problem (or an opportunity) and the determination to do something about it.

Margaret Knight was poor, uneducated and only 12 years old in 1850 when she saw a worker injured while weaving on a loom in a New Hampshire cotton mill. She invented a loom attachment to prevent future accidents. Margaret went on to invent many other things, including one we still use today—the flat-bottomed paper bag.

A good imagination helps, too. Leonardo da Vinci was born in Italy in 1452, yet his notebooks are stuffed with descriptions and drawings of modern inventions such as the automobile, helicopter and army tank. Unfortunately, Leonardo's ideas were so far ahead of his time that very few were ever built. Leonardo, by the way, was trained not as an inventor but as a painter.

Bytes

Velcro was invented by Swiss engineer George de Mestral in 1951. After a hike, he took a close look at the burrs that had stuck to his socks. The burrs had tiny hooks that latched onto loops in the fibers of the socks. His Velcro used the same principle of hooks and loops to attach things together.

Careless servants prompted American Josephine Cochrane to invent the dishwasher in 1886. She was tired of replacing dishes broken during washing and set out to invent a machine that could do a gentler job.

American Jim Wollin was only 14 when he invented a jar that could be opened from both ends so that you could get to the very last bit inside. He called it the Jar of Plenty.

Eureka!

FaQ **How do inventors invent?**

Fifteen-year-old Chester Greenwood's ears drove him to invent. In the winter of 1873, he got sick of freezing his ears while out skating. He bent some wire into a U-shape and asked his grandmother to sew beaver fur on the ends. The result was a new invention — earmuffs.

Like earmuffs, many inventions happen because people come across a problem and decide to fix it. Sometimes they have a brilliant idea and — eureka! — they invent something completely new.

More often inventors build on what others have tried before. The Wright brothers, for instance, spent years reading about other people's experiments with flight before they began their own. See page 22 for more about their invention.

And then there are the inventions that happen by accident. In 1878, a worker at Procter & Gamble took a lunch break and forgot to turn off the machine that mixed the soap. It just kept going, stirring in more and more air. Back on the job, the worker thought the batch of soap was ruined, but the soap had one unusual quality — it floated. Named Ivory, the soap was a hit with bathers tired of fumbling around for a bar in the bathwater.

Can inventing make you rich?

Bette Graham turned her poor typing skills into a fortune. She made so many mistakes that she had to invent a way to cover them up. The result was a white paint that covered errors, called Liquid Paper. At first she whipped up the stuff in her kitchen, but her business grew so much that she eventually sold it, in 1979, for the grand sum of $47.5 million.

But not all inventors become rich. Canadian Thomas Breakey invented the paint roller in 1940. The roller revolutionized house painting, but Breakey never made a dime from it. Others took his idea and profited instead.

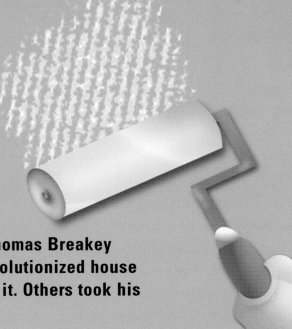

Bytes

The flash of inspiration that can lead to an invention is sometimes called the Eureka moment. Why? Long ago, when a Greek mathematician named Archimedes stepped into his bath, he had a flash of inspiration that allowed him to solve a problem. "Eureka!" he yelled. Translation: "I have found it!"

Percy Spencer only got as far as the fifth grade, but that didn't stop him from inventing. Over his lifetime, he received more than a hundred patents for his inventions, including one for the microwave oven.

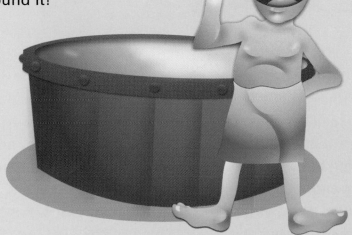

Everyday Inventions

FaQ

Why was money invented?

Like many inventions, money makes life easier. Say money hadn't been invented and you wanted a new skateboard. You'd have to trade something for it: for example, your pet rabbit. But what if the skateboard owner was allergic to rabbits? You'd have to find someone else who *did* want the rabbit and had something the skateboard owner wanted. With money, things are a lot simpler. You could sell the bunny and use the cash to buy the board.

Money in one form or another has been around for thousands of years. At first shells, beads and fishhooks were used as money. Then, nearly 2700 years ago, the king of Lydia (an ancient country in what is now Turkey) invented coins. They had his name on them and a guaranteed value, much like today's coins. Paper money was invented in ancient China in 802, and the credit card first appeared about 50 years ago.

FaQ

When was the pencil invented?

Back in about 1500, some English shepherds stumbled across a patch of dark rock and discovered it was great for making marks. Only one problem: the rock, later known as graphite, was so soft that it left messy smudges everywhere.

To keep their hands clean, people wrapped graphite in cloth, twigs, sheepskin, string— even wood. But the result was *still* messy. Finally, in 1795, a French engineer named Nicolas-Jacques Conté ground up some graphite, mixed it with clay to make it harder and less smudgy, and surrounded it with wood. The pencil was invented!

What were the first books like?

Definitely not something you'd want to take to bed with you. Books were long pieces of papyrus (mashed-up, flattened reeds) rolled into scrolls often as long as a school bus. Although scrolls were cumbersome, they were an improvement over the previous way of recording things — on heavy, easy-to-break stone tablets.

Scrolls, a 5000-year-old Egyptian invention, were replaced about 2000 years ago by a Roman invention. The Romans cut pages of parchment (tanned animal skins) and bound them together to form the first books.

Early books were written and copied by hand by monks, and it could take months or even years to copy a single book. All that changed with the printing press. First invented by the Chinese in the ninth century, the printing press didn't really catch on in the rest of the world until Johannes Gutenberg invented his own version in Germany in the 1440s.

Byte

In early books, wordswereruntogetherlikethis. Spaces between words weren't invented until about the tenth century.

Wearable Inventions

When was the zipper invented?

Zippers are only about 100 years old. American W.L. Judson came up with a "clasp locker or unlocker" that looked like today's zipper in early 1891. But it was for shoes, not clothes, and kept splitting open. In 1912, Swedish-born Gideon Sundback perfected the zipper and turned it into the clothes closer we know today.

How were sneakers invented?

Long ago, the Native people of Brazil came up with an ingenious way to protect bare feet. They cut a hole in a rubber tree, gathered some sap in a bowl, set it near a fire to keep the sap liquid, then dipped in their feet. When the sap hardened, they had rubber-soled feet. In 1832, an American named Wait Webster patented a way to attach rubber soles to shoes, and the sneaker was born.

Why was the safety pin invented?

Clothes have been around since the cave dwellers. But getting clothes to stay on was another matter. One solution was a pin that attached two pieces of clothing together. The ancient Romans called their pins *fibulae*, and some were as big as the palm of your hand. In 1849, American Walter Hunt invented the smaller version that won't spring open and stab you, rightly called the "safety" pin.

When was underwear invented?

Archaeologists in Iraq dug up a 5000-year-old statue of a girl wearing underpants, so we know underwear is at least that old. But elastic wasn't invented until 1820, by an Englishman named Thomas Hancock. How did people keep their underwear up before that? Here's your chance to invent your own underwear stayer-upper.

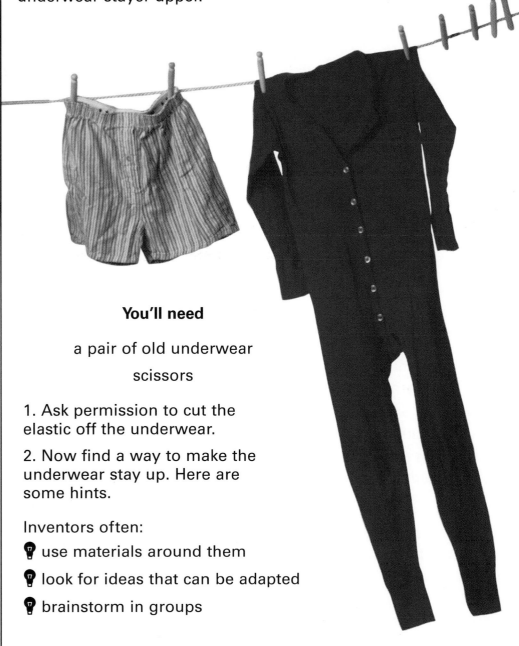

You'll need

a pair of old underwear

scissors

1. Ask permission to cut the elastic off the underwear.

2. Now find a way to make the underwear stay up. Here are some hints.

Inventors often:

💡 use materials around them

💡 look for ideas that can be adapted

💡 brainstorm in groups

Why were blue jeans invented?

When Levi Strauss went to the California gold rush in 1850, he quickly saw there was a need for pants that could withstand the wear and tear of digging for gold. Strauss used canvas to whip up some pants that wore like iron.

The only trouble was, miners' tools ripped the pockets. One tailor, sick of sewing on pockets, took a pair of pants to a blacksmith and, for a joke, had him reinforce the pockets with rivets. Take a look at your jeans — they may have the same rivets that started as a tailor's joke.

Around the House

When were houses invented?

Early humans didn't have houses; they simply sought shelter in caves. Then, about 40 000 years ago, some adventurous cave dwellers decided to move. When they found themselves in an area without caves, they dug a big shallow hole, crawled in and dragged branches or rocks into a circle around them. The pit house — the first shelter *for* people built *by* people — was invented.

Where was the lightbulb invented?

A light powered by electricity was such a great idea that several people were working on it at the same time. They were trying to find a way to send electricity through a wire to make it glow without burning up. One of them was the American Thomas Alva Edison. He tested thousands of materials. He also bought rights to other inventors' ideas, including those of two Canadians.

On the other side of the Atlantic, a British engineer named Joseph Swan came up with a working lightbulb in early 1879, just months before Edison. The two inventors sued each other, both claiming to be first. Then a lightbulb went on in the two men's minds. They ended their legal battle and set up a company together to manufacture their illuminating invention.

Byte

The lightbulb (page 12) and the telephone (page 33) were invented by two inventors at almost the same time. Creative minds often have the same bright idea when new materials or scientific discoveries open the door to new inventions.

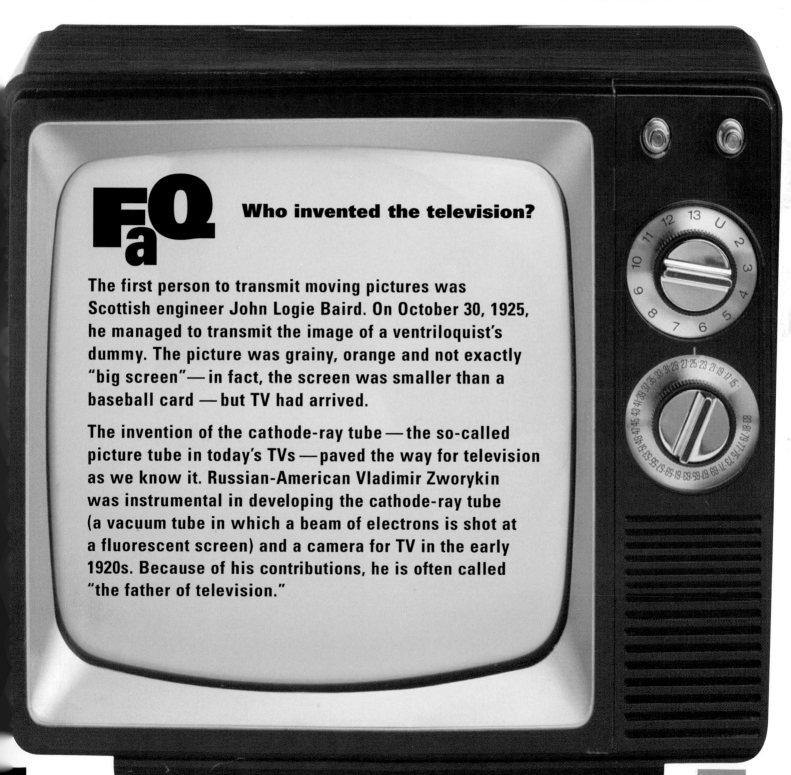

FaQ   Who invented the television?

The first person to transmit moving pictures was Scottish engineer John Logie Baird. On October 30, 1925, he managed to transmit the image of a ventriloquist's dummy. The picture was grainy, orange and not exactly "big screen"—in fact, the screen was smaller than a baseball card —but TV had arrived.

The invention of the cathode-ray tube —the so-called picture tube in today's TVs —paved the way for television as we know it. Russian-American Vladimir Zworykin was instrumental in developing the cathode-ray tube (a vacuum tube in which a beam of electrons is shot at a fluorescent screen) and a camera for TV in the early 1920s. Because of his contributions, he is often called "the father of television."

Where was the bathtub invented?

No one knows for sure, but the earliest bathtub found so far was at Knossos on the Greek island of Crete. This 4000-year-old tub looked a lot like what you might find in your bathroom today. But then the bathtub took a strange turn — it grew. By the early years of the first millennium, the Romans were building enormous baths and bathing became a public event. If you joined the crowd at the Baths of Caracalla in Rome, for instance, you could expect to take a bath with 1600 other people.

Who invented the toilet?

You may have heard of Thomas Crapper, who is often said to have invented the toilet. Crapper, a London plumber, *did* patent some toilet modifications in the early 1900s, but he didn't invent the toilet itself. That honor goes to Sir John Harrington, a nephew of Queen Elizabeth I, back in 1596. His toilet had a handle that you could pull to send water flushing through a basin.

The Harrington toilet was a big improvement, but it didn't catch on. People preferred cheaper chamber pots, even though they had to be dumped by hand. Finally, in 1775, a British inventor named Alexander Cummings developed an inexpensive and efficient toilet and started a bathroom revolution.

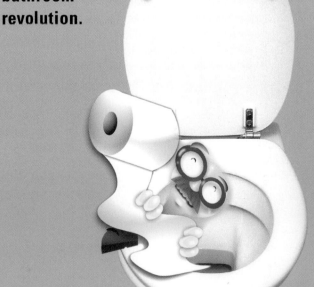

When were plates, knives and forks invented?

No one knows when plates were invented, but as late as the Middle Ages there still weren't many of them around. Instead, most people used trenchers. These were thick slabs of bread that stews and other foods were scooped onto. After eating the food, you were supposed to leave the bread trencher behind for the servants who did the cleaning up, or the dogs.

Knives have been around since prehistoric times, but they probably weren't used at the table until the Middle Ages. Then people started to carry their own knives with them and used them to both cut and spear food. Forks, which were invented in Byzantium (today known as Istanbul), caught on in Europe only in the mid-1500s. Some had two tines, others as many as five. Most people considered forks a new-fangled invention and wouldn't use them. They preferred their knives or, better still, their built-in cutlery—fingers.

Byte

Frances Gabe hated cleaning, so she invented a self-cleaning house. Soapy water sprayed from jets in the floor and ceiling, washing away dirt. (The furniture was waterproof.) Sound like sci-fi? Ms. Gabe built her own self-cleaning house in Newberg, Oregon, in 1955. Total cleaning time: one hour.

Fun and Games

When was chewing gum invented?

The Maya and Aztecs of Central America had been chewing chicle (the sap of the sapodilla tree) for hundreds of years before American Thomas Adams got the bright idea of forming it into balls and, in 1871, into sticks.

Later, the chicle sticks were chopped into bits and coated with candy. They were called little chicles, or Chiclets.

Are pets inventions?

Put a Chihuahua and a wolf together (make sure the wolf isn't hungry) and you'll see some basic similarities — tail, ears, four legs, etc. But you'll also notice some big differences. The Chihuahua, like all modern dogs, is an invention. Dog breeders started with the wolf thousands of years ago and, by selective breeding, came up with more than a hundred dog breeds.

The same is true for cats, goldfish and most pets. Thanks to pet inventors, we have furless cats, goldfish with lion-like manes and, yes, dogs small enough to fit in a teacup.

Bytes

In the 1870s, a tax collector in Germany needed a dog to guard the money he collected. Over several years, he bred ferocious dogs together to create a breed of superb guard dogs that was named after him. His name? Louis Dobermann.

American astronauts smuggled gum into space on the *Gemini 5* mission in 1965. To avoid getting caught with it when they returned to Earth, they did what kids have done for years: they swallowed it.

 ## Who invented the Frisbee?

A lot of people had a hand in inventing the Frisbee. It all started in a Connecticut bakery in 1871. Baker William Frisbie made pies in tins stamped with his name. Nearby college students would eat the pies and throw the tins, yelling "Frisbie" to avoid beaning anyone.

Cut to California in 1948. Fred Morrison decided to capitalize on people's fascination with aliens and flying saucers by making a throwable plastic disc. But he didn't have much luck with it until the Wham-O Company got involved. When Wham-O co-founder Rich Knerr heard about the tin Frisbie, he renamed (and re-spelled) his disc the Frisbee.

 ## Who invented basketball?

Michael Jordan owes it all to James Naismith, a Canadian working at a YMCA in Springfield, Massachusetts. Naismith needed a game that could be played indoors in cold weather, and so he invented one. In 1891, he nailed peach baskets up on the wall and got teams to try to toss a ball into the baskets to score points. These were the baskets that gave "basketball" its name.

Historians think a game like basketball was played by the Aztecs of Central America 1500 years ago. To play *Tlachtli*, as it was called, you shot a rubber ball through a stone hoop. But the game was played for religious purposes — and the losers were often sacrificed to the gods.

Edible Inventions

FaQ

Why was the sandwich invented?

The great thing about a sandwich is that you can hold it in one hand while you do something with the other. That's why the sandwich was invented —for convenience. Its inventor, John Montagu, was playing cards one day in 1762 when he got hungry. Instead of stopping for a meal, he slapped some food (probably meat) between two pieces of bread and ate as he played.

Montagu was one of those lucky inventors who had his invention named after him. His full name was John Montagu, fourth Earl of Sandwich.

FaQ

Who invented canned food?

An Englishman by the name of Bryan Donkin first rolled tin into a tube and sealed food in it. By 1812, he was "canning" fruit, vegetables, stews and soups. Canned food was popular with armies, explorers and others on the move and in need of easy-to-carry food.

Moo

William Parry took canned food with him as he explored the Arctic in 1824. When a can from his expedition was opened 112 years later, the veal inside was still edible.

Byte

The can opener wasn't invented until about 50 years after the can. Early cans were labeled: "Cut round on the top near to the outer edge with a chisel and hammer." Very, very messy.

Who invented the ice cream cone?

It was a hot summer day in 1904 when the ice cream cone was invented. A teenager named Arnold Fornachou was selling ice cream at the World's Fair in St. Louis, Missouri, and ran out of cups. Next to him was a baker who made waffles. Arnold borrowed a waffle, rolled it into a cone and plopped in some ice cream.

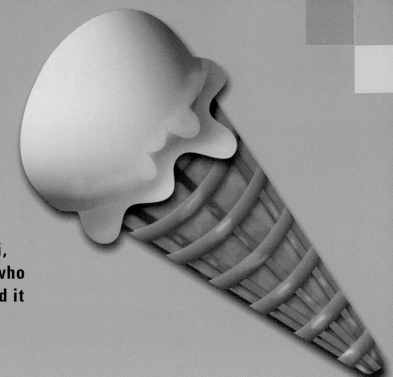

Can you really invent foods?

Most foods have been "invented." Over thousands of years, people looked for the healthiest food plants or the ones with the best-tasting fruits and bred them together. This "selective breeding" has produced new foods not found in nature. Today, the genes of plants can be altered to produce more food more economically. But not everyone agrees that these genetically modified foods are a good thing.

There's another way to invent foods — by combining existing foods in new ways. Ready to invent a new cookie?

You'll need

325 mL (1 1/2 c.) vanilla wafer crumbs

25 mL (2 tbsp.) corn syrup

50 mL (1/4 c.) juice concentrate (any flavor)

125 mL (1/2 c.) finely chopped dried fruits (any kind)

50 mL (1/4 c.) chopped nuts or seeds (any type)

a large bowl, a spoon

1. In the bowl, mix the crumbs and corn syrup.

2. This is where the inventing begins. Stir in the juice concentrate, dried fruits and nuts or seeds. Use whatever flavor combination you like. Grape-raisin-pumpkin?

3. Roll a spoonful of the dough into a ball. No baking required. Congratulations: you've just invented a new cookie.

On the Move

Who invented the wheel?

Unfortunately, the name of the inventor who got the whole world rolling has been lost in the mists of time. No wonder: the wheel was invented about 5500 years ago. Imagine how much easier it was to roll heavy loads (or have them pulled by oxen) instead of carrying them. Early wheels were solid wood and heavy until someone (whose name is lost, too!) cut away parts of the wheel, leaving spokes.

Who invented the bicycle?

A drawing from an Egyptian pyramid shows a man seated astride a bar that has a wheel attached at either end. He probably propelled it by pushing it with his feet. The ancient Chinese also had an early form of bicycle, but a bicycle with pedals wasn't invented until 1839, by a Scottish blacksmith named Kirkpatrick Macmillan. His pedals didn't go around — they went back and forth. Modern pedals appeared in the mid-1850s, and the bicycle craze took off.

But riding can't have been much fun until air-filled tires were invented by Scottish-born veterinarian John Dunlop in 1888. In fact, the jarring ride of early bicycles, with their wooden wheels and iron rims, earned them the name "boneshakers."

Kirkpatrick Macmillan's first pedal bicycle

How did cars get invented?

It depends on what you mean by "car." If a three-wheeled, steam-driven vehicle with a top speed of 4 km/h (2½ m.p.h.) fits the bill, then the first car was invented by French engineer Nicolas Cugnot in 1769.

An automobile with a gasoline-powered engine and four wheels wasn't invented until Germans Gottlieb Daimler and Wilhelm Maybach put their heads together in 1889.

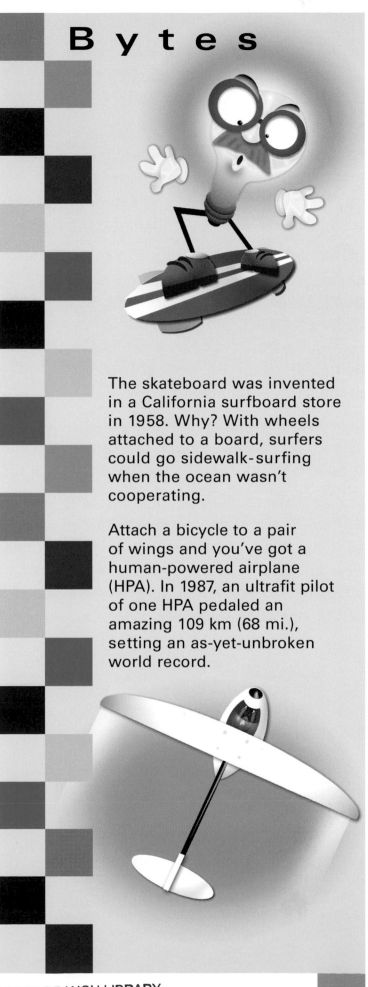

The skateboard was invented in a California surfboard store in 1958. Why? With wheels attached to a board, surfers could go sidewalk-surfing when the ocean wasn't cooperating.

Attach a bicycle to a pair of wings and you've got a human-powered airplane (HPA). In 1987, an ultrafit pilot of one HPA pedaled an amazing 109 km (68 mi.), setting an as-yet-unbroken world record.

FaQ How did airplanes get invented?

A famous myth tells about Icarus, whose wax and feather wings melted when he flew too close to the sun. Since myths often contain lessons, this one may have been trying to say, "Don't fool with Mother Nature—flying is for the birds."

Fortunately, that didn't stop early flight enthusiasts. In A.D. 875, an Arab named Abu'l-Qasim 'Abbas bin Firnas glued on vulture feathers, climbed a tall tower and jumped off. Onlookers say he flew for quite a distance, but most of it was probably straight down.

Inventors began experimenting with balloons, kites and gliders, but these flyers lacked power and control. Around the world, people tried to find the secret to sustained human flight.

In their hometown of Dayton, Ohio, the Wright brothers, Wilbur and Orville, began experimenting with controls, wing shapes and engine designs. Almost 10 years of thinking and tinkering came together near Kitty Hawk, North Carolina, on December 17, 1903, when their airplane, *The Flyer*, flew into aviation history with a flight that lasted a brief 12 seconds.

Byte

The first flight of the Wright brothers' plane could have taken place *inside* a Boeing 747, with plenty of room to spare.

The only way is to try it, again and again. When the Wright brothers were searching for the perfect shape for an airplane wing, they tested more than 200 wing shapes. Try making this flyer out of a Styrofoam tray and see what you can discover about wing shapes.

You'll need

3 or more supermarket Styrofoam trays

scissors, tape

1. Cut a triangle out of one Styrofoam tray. The triangle can be any shape or size. Cut a slot in the back of the triangle as shown. This is the wing of your flyer.

2. Cut a right-angle triangle out of the other Styrofoam tray. Cut a slot as shown Snip off the tip. This is the rudder.

3. Slip the rudder into the slot on the wing, tape it lightly in place and see how your flyer flies.

4. Keep experimenting with wing shapes and sizes (step 1) until you find one that lets your flyer really soar.

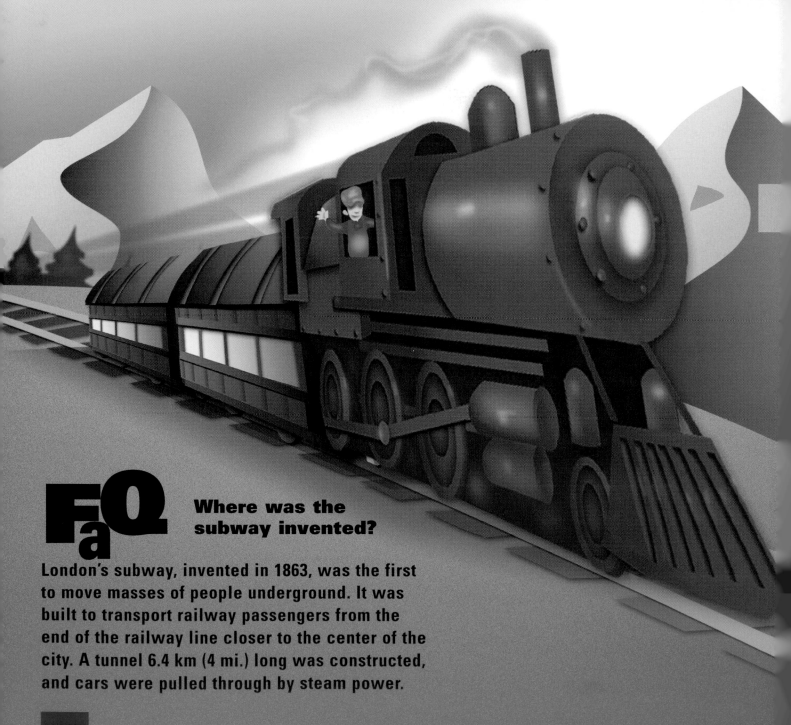

 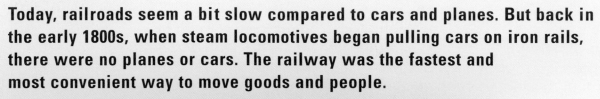

Why were railroads invented?

Today, railroads seem a bit slow compared to cars and planes. But back in the early 1800s, when steam locomotives began pulling cars on iron rails, there were no planes or cars. The railway was the fastest and most convenient way to move goods and people.

No one is sure who first came up with the idea of rails, but there are records of mine carts on wooden rails in Alsace (eastern France) in 1556.

Where was the subway invented?

London's subway, invented in 1863, was the first to move masses of people underground. It was built to transport railway passengers from the end of the railway line closer to the center of the city. A tunnel 6.4 km (4 mi.) long was constructed, and cars were pulled through by steam power.

Who invented the submarine?

A Dutchman named Cornelis Drebbel first tested a submarine in England's Thames River in the early 1620s. His waterproof wooden boat held a crew of 12 men, who breathed through tubes leading up to the surface. In repeated tests, the submarine reached depths of 4.6 m (15 ft.) and could stay under for up to three hours. Amazingly, the men rowed the submarine around with oars.

When was the compass invented?

Planes and trains and automobiles — if you're on the move it helps to know where you are. Enter the compass. It was invented in China in about 1100. The inventor's name is lost, but thanks to this invention, travelers aren't.

Why were rockets invented?

Rockets weren't invented to explore space — they were invented as weapons. The Chinese used arrows attached to tiny rockets powered by gunpowder (another Chinese invention) in warfare almost a thousand years ago. But until World War II, rockets weren't reliable — some hit the target, but most didn't.

Using rockets for space travel didn't happen until October 4, 1957, when the Soviet Union used a rocket to boost the satellite *Sputnik I* into space. Since then more than 4000 rockets have lifted off.

Medical Marvels

When was the X-ray invented?

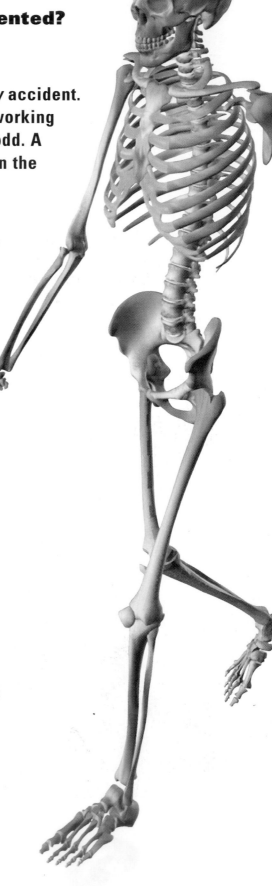

The X-ray, so useful *after* an accident, happened *by* accident. A German physicist named Wilhelm Röntgen was working late one night in 1895 when he noticed something odd. A piece of paper with a fluorescent coating glowed in the dim light. It was near a tube where he had been experimenting with cathode rays.

Röntgen was mystified. The tube was covered with cardboard and tinfoil, so the cathode rays could not escape it. He wondered if some new kind of rays were coming from the tube, striking the paper and making it glow. Weeks of experiments convinced him that there *were* mysterious rays, which he called X-rays — "X" stands for the unknown.

Röntgen discovered that the X-rays could penetrate flesh to show the bones below. He became famous and won the first Nobel prize for physics.

Byte

We usually think of X-raying bodies, but Dorothy Crowfoot Hodgkin had another idea. In 1964 she won a Nobel Prize for X-raying molecules of penicillin, vitamins and insulin. Her work helped researchers develop new drugs.

FaQ

Where and when were eyeglasses invented?

No one knows for certain where eyeglasses were invented. By A.D. 1100, monks in Europe were using a "reading stone," a primitive magnifying glass, to help them copy and illustrate books. Italian glassmakers figured out how to make basic glass lenses, and by the latter half of the 1200s, two lenses were attached together and perched on the nose.

FaQ

Who invented Band-Aids?

We have Earle Dickson's wife to thank for Band-Aids. She was accident prone and often ended up with cuts or burns. Earle Dickson worked for Johnson & Johnson, a company making antiseptic bandages for hospitals. But the hospital bandages were too large for his wife's cuts, so Dickson snipped off a small piece and attached it to a strip of adhesive tape. He used crinoline fabric to cover the adhesive to keep it from sticking to things until it was needed.

Johnson & Johnson started to manufacture the tiny adhesive bandages in 1921 in New Brunswick, New Jersey. But no one else showed any interest until the company offered free samples to Boy Scout troops. It seemed the Boy Scouts were as accident prone as Mrs. Dickson, and Band-Aids took off.

Stuff

Who invented paper?

A Chinese court official named Ts'ai Lun is thought to have invented paper in A.D. 105. He mashed up some wet hemp, rags and old fish nets, then drained off the water. The result was paper. Later, shredded rags were used in the papermaking process.

Although the Chinese tried to keep papermaking a secret so that they alone could profit from it, some Chinese papermakers were kidnapped by Arabs in 751, and the technology of papermaking gradually spread to the rest of the world.

The paper in this book, like most modern paper, is made of wood fibers. Canadian Charles Fenerty came up with the idea in 1838 after seeing wasps making paper nests out of wood. He went home, ground up some wood, mixed it with water and invented the first paper created completely out of wood fiber.

When was glass invented?

Glass was invented about 4500 years ago in Mesopotamia, an ancient country located in present-day Iraq. At first, glass was used mostly for beads and other decorations. Then, just over 2000 years ago, people in the Middle East learned how to blow molten glass into bowls or vases.

The ancient Romans excelled at glass blowing and eventually figured out a way to make window glass. Around A.D. 100, glass windows, although still hazy by today's standards, were showing up in Rome's important buildings and the villas of the rich.

FaQ

Who invented concrete?

Mix together sand, rocks and cement, add some water and you've got concrete, the material that modern roads and buildings depend on. It was the ancient Romans who first came up with a concrete-like mixture. They used it to build aqueducts (water-transporting structures), buildings and roads. Lots of roads. Their concrete roads across Europe measured 8530 km (5300 mi.), more than the 6760 km (4200 mi.) of U.S. interstate highways today.

The Romans' concrete recipe had some unusual ingredients, including horsehair, to prevent shrinkage as the concrete hardened.

Bytes

Inventors sometimes use new materials in unexpected ways. Take the concrete canoe, for example. The American Society of Civil Engineers sponsors an annual concrete canoe building competition. Participants have to paddle their canoe when it's finished.

When American chemist Spence Silver invented a glue that stuck things together only temporarily, everyone thought it was useless. Then, in 1974, Silver's co-worker Arthur Fry had a brainwave. Maybe the glue could be applied to paper to make *removable* notes. The result was Post-it Notes.

Where was rubber invented?

The Native people of Brazil were first to use rubber, to protect their feet (see page 10). By the early 1800s, rubber was being shipped to America. It seemed promising, but it was sticky in summer and cracked in winter.

Charles Goodyear was intrigued by rubber. He was convinced it could stay pliable year-round if a softener was mixed with it. For years he tried adding chemicals, ink and even soup, but nothing worked.

Then, in 1839, he accidentally dropped a blob of rubber mixed with sulfur on the stove. Goodyear tested the rubber by nailing it outside, to the wall of his house. Amazingly, it didn't crack in the cold. He called the process he had invented vulcanization after Vulcan, the Roman god of fire.

When was plastic invented?

About 150 years ago, a British professor sold his patent for a new material to John Hyatt of Albany, New York. Hyatt entered the stuff, which he called Celluloid, in a contest to find a replacement for ivory billiard balls and it won. Celluloid, the first plastic material, was impressive stuff, except that it twisted and melted when heated.

A new material called Bakelite solved that problem. Invented by a Belgian-American named Leo Baekeland in 1907, it soon became even more popular than Celluloid. It was the grandfather of the plastics we have today.

Are new materials still being invented?

Every few years, a new material comes along. In 1964, for example, American chemist Stephanie Kwolek turned an accident in a lab into a new kind of plastic. The stuff was super strong — five times stronger than the same weight of steel. Named Kevlar, it's now used for lots of things, including bulletproof vests that can stop a bullet from 3 m (10 ft.) away.

Here's your chance to figure out a use for a material you can make in your kitchen.

You'll need

a box of cornstarch

a large cake pan

a spoon

water

food coloring (optional)

1. Empty the cornstarch into the cake pan.

2. With the spoon, stir in the water bit by bit until your mixture is the thickness of mayonnaise. Add a bit of food coloring if you wish.

3. Now do some testing:

💡 Slap your hand into the stuff. Is it a liquid or a solid?

💡 Pick some up and hold it in your hands. Roll it into a ball. What happens when you stop rolling?

💡 Pinch some between your fingers, then let go.

What would you call the stuff? How could you use it?

Store your invention in an airtight plastic container or throw it in the garbage. Do not pour it down the sink or toilet — it can cause clogs.

In Touch

When was mail delivery invented?

Messages were one of the earliest forms of communications. They were delivered by human runner, horseback messenger or even pigeon. But it was Cyrus the Great of Persia, an ancient kingdom in the Middle East, who put together an organized system for the delivery of messages around 530 B.C.

Cyrus figured out how far a horse could travel in one day, then built stations where horse and rider could rest or, if necessary, be replaced. The Romans borrowed this early postal system, and gradually more and more people began to communicate by mail.

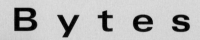

Bytes

The ancient Romans sometimes used dogs to carry messages. The dogs were made to swallow a small tube containing a message, and then their stomachs were slit open at their destination to retrieve the message.

In 1971, American Erna Schneider Hoover figured out how to relieve overloaded telephone switchboards with her computerized switching system. She received one of the first software patents.

Burp!

Who invented the telephone?

Alexander Graham Bell and Elisha Gray raced to find a way to transmit voices electronically over a wire. Bell applied for a patent for the telephone just two hours before Gray. Years of lawsuits followed as the courts tried to sort out who was the rightful inventor. In the end, Alexander Graham Bell won.

Bell's idea was that the voice would make a metal disc vibrate, and its vibrations could change the intensity of an electric current. To hear the sound, the process had only to be reversed: the changing electric current would cause a disc to vibrate, which would send the vibrations to the ear.

Sounds simple, but it took years of experimenting, with lots of failures along the way. Then, on March 10, 1876, theory became reality. Bell, who had spilled acid on his pants, shouted into the mouthpiece of his telephone, "Mr. Watson — Come here — I want to see you." To his astonishment, Watson ran in from another room. Communication had instantly become instant.

F a Q

Why was the cell phone invented?

People on the move, such as cabbies, truck drivers and police, had a big interest in phones that didn't have to be plugged in. But inventors had a hunch that other people might find a portable phone useful, too, and the race was on to invent one. In 1973, American Martin Cooper made the first phone call from a portable phone. He called his competitors to tell them he'd done it.

Who invented the computer?

The earliest computers were more like calculators. Then, in the 1830s, an English mathematician named Charles Babbage came up with an idea for a machine that could process data (information). Unfortunately, it was so far ahead of its time that it was never built.

It took more than a hundred years for technology to catch up with Babbage's idea. The first computers as we know them were developed in the 1940s. One of the earliest, the Colossus, helped Britain decode intercepted German messages during World War II.

Early computers weren't exactly desktop models. The Mark I, developed at Harvard University in 1944, measured 15.5 m (51 ft.) long and weighed almost as much as an African elephant.

When was the Internet invented?

The idea for a network of linked computers started in the late 1960s. The U.S. Defense Department wanted to make sure that data could be sent from one computer to another in case of Soviet attack. (This was when relations between the United States and the Soviet Union were tense.) And scientists at universities scattered around the United States wanted to share information and expensive computer time.

The first communication between computers in different places happened on October 29, 1969, when data were sent from one California university computer to another. Soon more university and defense department computers were linked. The Internet, as it is now called, grew by leaps and bounds. In the late 1990s, Internet traffic doubled every 100 days.

Who invented e-mail?

If you think of e-mail as messages sent electrically, then Samuel Morse would get the honor. In the 1830s, he came up with a way to turn off an electric signal for very short periods of time (dots) or slightly longer periods (dashes). Then he gave every letter a dot-dash code. For example:

f = • • — •   a = • —   q = — — • —

Using the code he invented, Morse could send a message over the telegraph, another one of his inventions.

Computer e-mail was invented by American Ray Tomlinson in late 1971. He can't remember the first message, although he thinks it might have been QWERTYIOP, a stringing together of most of the letters on the top row of the keyboard.

How does e-mail get sent?

E-mailing is a bit like chopping a letter into equal-sized bits (in computerese, these are called packets), mailing them at different mailboxes and trusting the post office to put them back together at the other end before delivering the letter to its destination.

Amazingly, the packets in one message don't all go the same route, but thanks to a numbered code attached to each packet, they always get reassembled at the right address and in the right order.

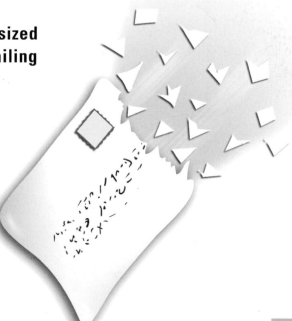

Are you Inventive?

FaQ Can kids invent?

Check out Jim Wollin and Margaret Knight (page 5), or Chester Greenwood (page 6). They're all kid-inventors. But there are lots more inventive kids out there. Here are just a few of them:

• At age 7, American Suzanna Gooden invented the edible pet spoon, made out of a dog biscuit. No more messy washing up after Fido.

• Nine-year-old Austin Meggitt of Ohio invented a holder for a baseball bat, glove and ball that could be attached to a bicycle to make the ride to the baseball field safer. His "Glove and Battie Caddie" got him inducted into the National Inventors Hall of Fame in 1999.

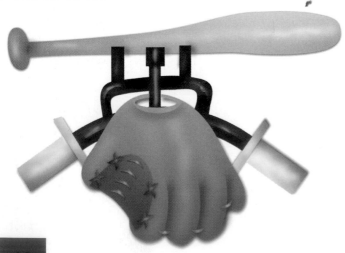

• Grade 6 student Elizabeth Armstrong of Ontario invented "Eek A Bug!" to remove bugs from the house. It's a long tube equipped with a plunger. Pull the plunger and air pressure sucks up the bug so that you can deposit it outside.

• In 1922, 15-year-old Quebecer Armand Bombardier turned an old car into the first snowmobile. Today, Bombardier snowmobiles are the way to go when the snow falls.

• California tenth-grade student Krysta Morlan had to spend months with casts on both legs. To relieve that sweaty, itchy-under-the-plaster feeling, she invented a way to pump cool air under the cast called the Cast Cooler.

WHEW!

How do you keep people from stealing your invention?

Inventors apply for patents to protect their inventions. A patent is a legal document that says no one else can profit from your invention without your permission for many years.

Kids *have* been granted patents for their inventions. So if you think you've come up with a brand-new invention (a pencil-calculator to speed up math homework?) or even an improvement to an existing invention (ice skates with brakes?), go for it. Type in "Patent Office" on any Internet search engine for information on how to apply for a patent in your country.

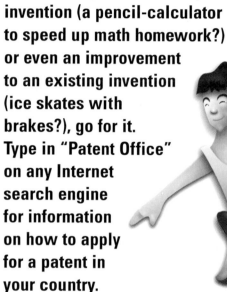

B y t e

Not all inventions are useful. In fact, some are downright silly. For instance, inventors have invented a contraption to help you twiddle your thumbs and a machine to scramble an egg — in the shell. Anything's possible, when the urge to invent strikes.

FaQ

Are there still things left to invent?

Someone once said, "Whenever man comes up with a better mousetrap, nature immediately comes up with a better mouse." We have to keep inventing — to stay ahead — to save lives, time, energy, money — or just to have fun.

You are part of the next generation of inventors. So here's your chance. Look for a problem that's been bugging you and see what you can come up with to fix it. Once you've invented something new, you might want to show the world. Look for invention conventions, camps, fairs and contests in your area. Happy inventing!

Time Line

Date	Invention	Page
prehistory	the dog	16
prehistory	the house	12
about 3500 B.C.	the wheel	20
about 3000 B.C.	the cat	16
about 3000 B.C.	underwear	11
about 2500 B.C.	glass	28
about 2000 B.C.	the bathtub	14
about 700 B.C.	coins	8
about 530 B.C.	message delivery, which led to mail service	32
about 300 B.C.	concrete for roads and buildings	29
about A.D. 1	the book	9
about 100	the glass window	28
105	paper	28
about 500	*Tlachtli*, an Aztec game resembling basketball	17
802	paper money	8
about 1000	the goldfish	16
about 1000	the plate (for food)	15
about 1000	printing in China	9
about 1000	the table knife	15
about 1100	the compass	25
about 1100	the "reading stone," an early magnifying glass	27
1200s	eyeglasses with frames	27
1440s	Gutenberg's printing press	9
1550s	the table fork	15
1556	the railway	24
1596	the toilet	14

Date	Invention	Page
1620s	the submarine	25
1762	the sandwich	18
1769	the automobile	21
1795	the pencil	8
1812	canned food	18
1820	elastic	11
1830s	early computers	34
1830s	the telegraph and Morse code	35
1832	sneakers	10
1838	paper made of wood fibers	28
1839	the pedal bicycle	20
1839	vulcanized rubber	30
1849	the safety pin	10
1850	blue jeans	11
about 1860	the can opener	18
1863	the subway	24
1867	the paper bag (with flat bottom)	5
1870s	the Doberman Pinscher	16
1871	chewing gum in sticks	16
1873	earmuffs	6
1876	the telephone	33
1878	Ivory soap	6
1879	the lightbulb	12
1886	dishwasher	5
1888	the air-filled bicycle tire	20
1891	basketball	17
1891	early zipper	10
1895	the X-ray	26

Index

Doberman Pinscher dogs, 16
dogs, 16, 32
Donkin, Bryan, 18
Drebbel, Cornelis, 25
Dunlop, John, 20

Earl of Sandwich. *See* John Montagu
earmuffs, 6
Edison, Thomas Alva, 12
Egyptian inventions, ancient, 9, 20
elastic, 11
e-mail, 35
eyeglasses, 27

Fenerty, Charles, 28
fibulae (clothes fasteners), 10
food, 18–19
forks, 15
Fornachou, Arnold, 19
Frisbees, 17
Frisbie, William, 17
Fry, Arthur, 29

Gabe, Frances, 15
games, 17
genetically modified foods, 19
glass, 27, 28
goldfish, 16
Goodyear, Charles, 30
Graham, Bette, 7
Gray, Elisha, 33
Greek inventions, ancient, 7, 14
Greenwood, Chester, 6, 36
Gutenberg, Johannes, 9

Hancock, Thomas, 11
Harrington, Sir John, 14
Hodgkin, Dorothy Crowfoot, 26
Hoover, Erna Schneider, 32
household inventions, 12–13
houses, 12, 15
human-powered airplanes, 21
Hunt, Walter, 10
Hyatt, John, 30

ice cream cones, 19
Internet, 34
Ivory soap, 6

jars, 5
Judson, W.L., 10

Kevlar, 31
Knerr, Rich, 17

Knight, Margaret, 5, 36
knives, 15
Kwolek, Stephanie, 31

lightbulbs, 12, 13
Liquid Paper, 7
Lun, Ts'ai, 28

Macmillan, Kirkpatrick, 20
magnifying glasses, 27
mail delivery, 32
Maybach, Wilhelm, 21
medical inventions, 26–27
microwave ovens, 7
Middle Eastern inventions, ancient,
     8, 11, 15, 28, 32
money, 8
Montagu, John, 18
Morrison, Fred, 17
Morse, Samuel, 35

Naismith, James, 17
National Inventors Hall of Fame, 36
Native peoples, 10, 16, 17, 30
Nobel prizes, 26

paint rollers, 7
pants, 11
paper, 28
paper bags, 5
Parry, William, 18
patents, 7, 32, 37
pencils, 8
pets, 16
plastics, 30, 31
plates, 15
Post-it Notes, 29
printing, 9

railroads, 24
rockets, 25
Roman inventions, ancient, 9, 10,
     28, 29, 32
Röntgen, Wilhelm, 26
rubber, 10, 30

safety pins, 10
sandwiches, 18
selective breeding, 16, 19
Silver, Spence, 29
skateboards, 21
sneakers, 10
snowmobiles, 36
soap, 6

software, 32
Spencer, Percy, 7
Strauss, Levi, 11
submarines, 25
subways, 24
Sundback, Gideon, 10
Swan, Joseph, 12

telephones, 13, 33
televisions, 13
Tlachtli, 17
toilets, 14
Tomlinson, Ray, 35
transportation
     airplanes, 21, 22, 23
     automobiles, 21
     bicycles, 20, 21
     canoes, 29
     railroads, 24
     skateboards, 21
     snowmobiles, 36
     space rockets, 25
     submarines, 25
     subways, 24
     wheels, 20

underwear, 11

Velcro, 5
vulcanization, 30

Webster, Wait, 10
wheels, 20
women inventors, 5, 7, 15, 26, 31, 32
Wright, Orville and Wilbur, 6, 22, 23

X-rays, 26

zippers, 10
Zworykin, Vladimir, 13